Praise & Worship Favorites

Arranged for Two-part Choir

by Marty Parks

Lillenas PUBLISHING COMPANY

KANSAS CITY, MO 64141

CONTENTS

Lord, I Lift Your Name on High

Words and Music by
RICK FOUNDS
Arr. by Marty Parks

From the earth____ to the cross____ my____ debt to pay;__

From the cross____ to the grave,____ from the grave____ to the sky;__

Lord, I lift Your name__ on high!

7

8

Holy Ground

Words and Music by
GERON DAVIS
Arr. by Marty Parks

14

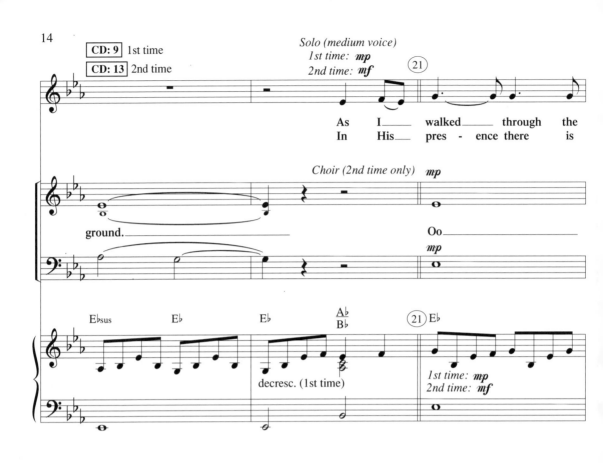

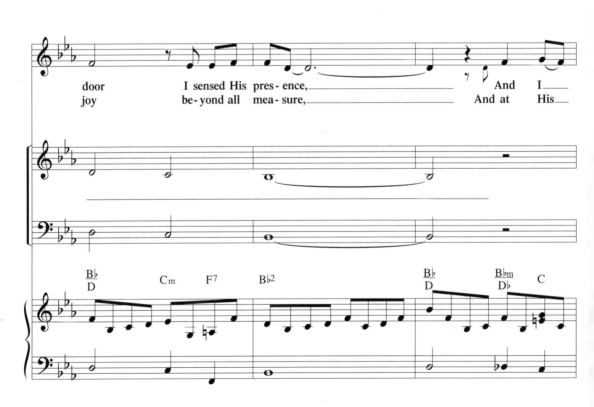

18

CD: 16

This Is My Prayer

with
Change My Heart, O God

Words and Music by
Doug Holck
Arr. by Marty Parks

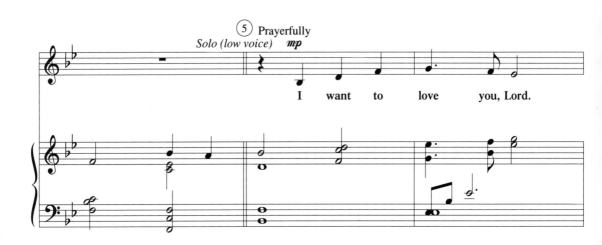

I want to love you, Lord.

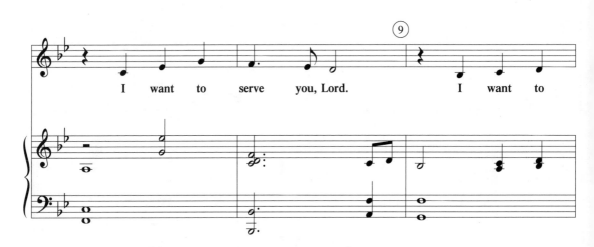

I want to serve you, Lord. I want to

41 *"Change My Heart, O God" (Eddie Espinosa)

Change my heart, O God,

Make it ev - er true.

Change my heart, O God,

May I be like You.

26

Great and Wonderful

Sing unto the Lord
Great and Wonderful
The Trees of the Field

Arr. by Marty Parks

28

30

CD: 29

32

34

*"The Trees of the Field" (Rubin/Dauermann)

lu - jah!   A - men! _____   You

shall   go   out   with joy____ and be led forth   with peace.__

The moun-tains and the   hills   shall   break forth   be -

36 (handclaps)

The trees of the field will clap their hands;

The trees of the field will clap their hands;

While you go out with joy! And all the

More Precious

More Precious than Silver
O Lord, You're Beautiful
Desire of My Heart

Arr. by Marty Parks

6 *"More Precious than Silver" (Lynn DeShazo)

Lord, You are more pre-cious than sil-ver, Lord, You are more cost-ly than

42

Be Exalted

Be Exalted, O God
The Heavens Declare

Arr. by Marty Parks

*"Be Exalted, O God"
(Brent Chambers)

48

49

50

glo - ry be o - ver all the earth.

*"The Heavens Declare"
(Doug Holck)

Choir unison *mp*

The heav - ens de -

55

We Trust in the Name of the Lord Our God

Words and Music by
STEVEN CURTIS CHAPMAN
Arr. by Marty Parks

CD: 57

name will_____ al - ways pre- vail;_____ We trust_____ in the name of the Lord our

God._____ Some trust_____ in the work they do, We

trust in the name of the Lord our God. By His grace___ all the work is thro', We

60

CD: 59

God. _____ His love nev - er fails, His

name will ___ al - ways pre - vail; ___

(drum fill)

We trust ___ in the name, We trust ___ in the name,

Jesus, I Love You

Lifting Up My Voice
My Jesus, I Love Thee
Fairest Lord Jesus

Arr. by Marty Parks

65

66

70

In the Presence of Jehovah

Words and Music by
GERON DAVIS
Arr. by Marty Parks

74

CD: 74

King.

Thro' His love the Lord pro - vid - ed_____ a place for us to rest;_____ A place to find the an - swer_____ in hours__ of dis-

I Will Worship You

Doxology
In Spirit and in Truth

Arr. by Marty Parks

82

83

21 *"In Spirit and in Truth" (Charlie Peacock)

Fa - ther, I will hon - or You in all I say and all I do; Fa - ther, I will wor - ship You in spir - it and in truth.

84

CD: 81

The Blood of Jesus

O the Blood of Jesus
Nothing But the Blood
We Shall Overcome

Arr. by Marty Parks

88

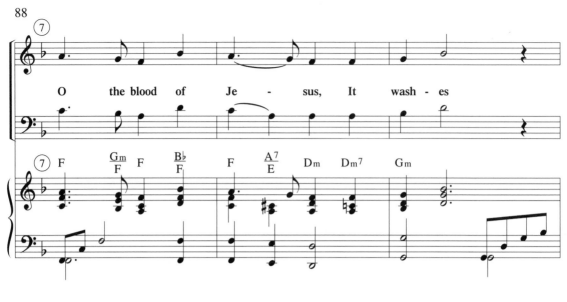

O the blood of Je - sus, It wash - es

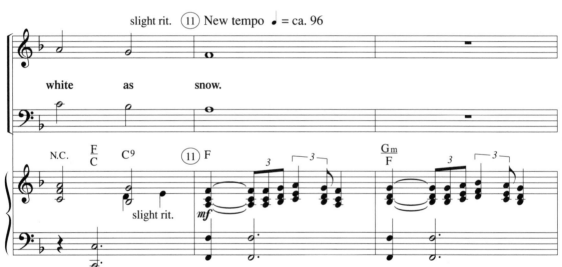

white as snow.

slight rit. ⑪ New tempo ♩ = ca. 96

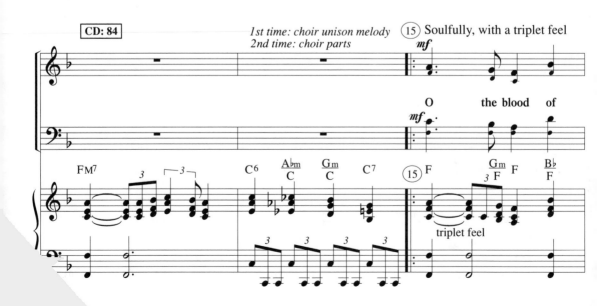

CD: 84

1st time: choir unison melody
2nd time: choir parts

⑮ Soulfully, with a triplet feel

O the blood of

*"Nothing But the Blood" (Robert Lowry)

90

*"We Shall Overcome" (Jack Hayford)

94

O the Glory of Your Presence

with
I Stand in Awe

Words and Music by
STEVE FRY
Arr. by Marty Parks

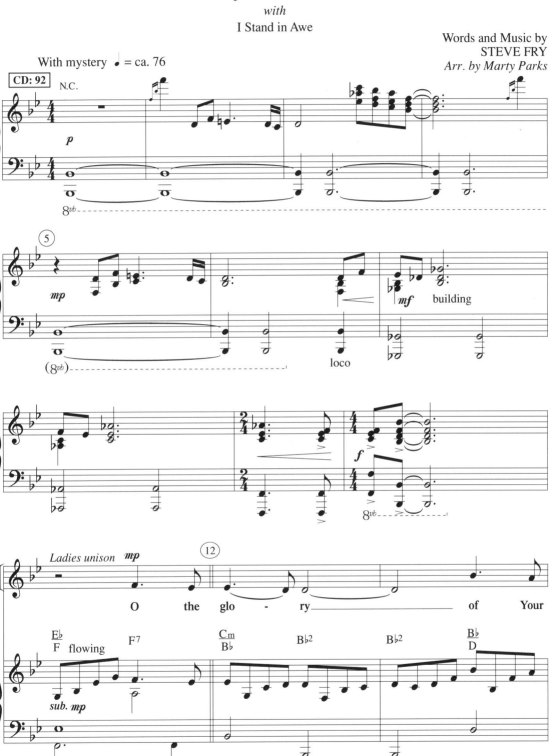

98

100

place. And I stand, I stand in

awe of You. I stand, I stand in awe of You. Ho-ly

God, to whom all praise is due, I stand in awe of